CAN YOU SEE WHAT I MEAN?

Sydney R. Finley

CAN YOU SEE WHAT I MEAN?

The comedian says "Do you see what I mean?'. *Can You See What I Mean?* provides these exercises to develop, hone or strengthen the skills necessary to "see", or, to establish the ability to perceive.. They are also designed to arouse curiosity such that one is able to strengthen processing skills, namely,

Listening skills   *Visualization skills*

Making connections   *Paying attention to detail*

At least 50% of the words being employed should be in a third grader's vocabulary, but these exercises can help anyone from any walk of life, from nine to ninety-nine, English language and foreign language speaker alike.

They offer a challenge to anyone and everyone, even the technologically challenged.

One can create one's own working environment, from competitive to leisurely to laissez-faire.

These are truly interactive exercises, as we recommend that you work with a partner, whether it is a parent or a peer.

One cannot develop skills without doing the activities!

It is easy to check all responses with the use of a dictionary.

The only limit is one's imagination.

New concepts are introduced by using prefixes and suffixes phonics, syllabication, comparison and other methods and before your very eyes, known concepts morph into new and different ones creating many new links with each other, thus spurring the player to do further research. Our players say "wow", as they experience both a sense of achievement and a sense of humility.

Bon Voyage on your journey of discovery and self-discovery.

Can You See What I Mean? boosts Social, Emotional, Educational and Industrial skills. In as little as 10 minutes per day, you'll feel the difference. It's not Science Fiction. You ***will*** feel the difference.

INSTRUCTIONS

Read all words aloud

Work with a partner

USE A DICTIONARY

for confirmation
to answer queries
to settle disputes

HETERONYMS

These are words that have identical spelling, but different sounds and meanings.

Write a description of the sentences listed below, explaining the meanings and part of speech of the word that seems to be repeated.

She analyses everything, and sometimes makes copies of her analyses.

They were fishing for bass when they heard the bass drum.

He moped as he rolled out his damaged moped.

It is a single use shaver, do not use it more than once.

Do not intimate that they have an intimate relationship.

Let me get closer to see the closer.

Homonyms and homophones help build many social skills, including listening. A renowned British playwright once complained that *fish,* may, in all sensibility be spelt *ghoti* (*gh* as in *tough, o,* as in *women, and ti,* as in *nation.* *Fishing* and *phishing* also have the same sound. Read all words aloud, then, Write a description of each of the pairs of words in the spaces provided.

acetic_____

ascetic_____

aid_____

aide_____

ail_____

ale_____

aisle_____

isle_____

albumen_____

albumin _____

all_____

awl _____

alms _____

arms _____

altar _____

alter _____

arc _____

ark _____

ashore _____

assure _____

ant _____

aunt _____

ante _____

auntie _____

arterial _____

arteriole _____

ascent _____

assent _____

auger _____

augur _____

aural _____

oral _____

axel _____

axle _____

bad _____

bade _____

bait _____

bate_____

bologna _____

baloney_____

bard _____

barred_____

bark_____

barque _____

base_____

bass _____

beach _____

beech _____

bean _____

been _____

beat _____

beet _____

bell _____

belle _____

berry _____

bury _____

berth _____

birth _____

bloc _____

block _____

blond _____

blonde _____

bogie _____

bogey _____

boos _____

booze _____

bootie _____

booty _____

bollocks _____

bullocks _____

bough_____

bow_____

boy _____

buoy _____

braise _____

brays_____

breach _____

breech _____

bread _____

bred _____

breadth_____

breath_____

breach _____

breech _____

bridal _____

bridle _____

broach _____

brooch _____

broth _____

brought _____

burger _____

burgher _____

cache _____

cash _____

call _____

caul _____

callous _____

callus _____

canter _____

cantor _____

canvas _____

canvass _____

capital _____

capitol _____

carat _____

carrot _____

carcase _____

carcass _____

carrion _____

carry-on _____

cast _____

caste _____

cause _____

caws _____

ceiling _____

sealing _____

chair _____

cheer _____

chanty _____

shanty _____

chase _____

chaise _____

chased _____

chaste _____

cereal _____

serial _____

cession _____

session _____

chilli _____

chilly _____

choir _____

quire _____

choral _____

chorale _____

chute _____

shoot _____

clause _____

claws _____

climb _____

clime _____

coach _____

couch _____

coarse _____

course _____

coif _____

quaff _____

coir _____

core _____

colonel _____

kernel _____

comedian _____

comedienne _____

complement _____

compliment _____

confectionary _____

confectionery _____

cops _____

copse _____

coral _____

corral _____

chord _____

cord _____

coo _____

coup _____

core _____

corps _____

council _____

counsel _____

crews _____

cruise _____

crotch _____

crutch _____

cue _____

queue _____

currant _____

current _____

cymbals _____

symbols _____

dais _____

days _____

dam _____

damn _____

dare _____

deer _____

defer _____

differ _____

defuse _____

diffuse _____

dew _____

due _____

discreet _____

discrete _____

discus _____

discuss _____

die _____

dye _____

does _____

doze _____

dollop _____

doll-up _____

douse _____

dowse _____

earn _____

urn _____

eider _____

either _____

eminent _____

imminent _____

emigrant _____

immigrant _____

faint _____

feint _____

fate _____

faith_____

father _____

farther_____

feat _____

feet _____

ferment_____

foment _____

flea _____

flee _____

floes_____

flows _____

flour _____

flower _____

fore _____

four _____

fork _____

falk _____

fort _____

forth _____

formally _____

formerly _____

gaff _____

gaffe _____

gamble _____

gambol _____

gait _____

gate _____

genes _____

jeans _____

goiter _____

goitre _____

gnus _____

noose _____

gorilla _____

guerilla _____

gourd _____

gourde _____

gray _____

grey _____

groan _____

grown _____

groin _____

groyne _____

guise _____

guys _____

hall _____

haul _____

hangar _____

hanger _____

hart _____

heart _____

haves _____

halves _____

heal _____

heel _____

heroin _____

heroine _____

higher _____

hire _____

hoar _____

whore _____

hoard _____

horde _____

hole _____

whole _____

isle _____

aisle _____

jam _____

jamb _____

knave _____

nave _____

knew _____

new _____

knight _____

night _____

knot _____

not _____

know _____

no _____

knows _____

nose _____

laps _____

lapse _____

larva _____

lava _____

lays _____

laze _____

lead _____

led _____

lessen _____

lesson _____

levee _____

levy _____

lean _____

lien _____

lichen _____

liken _____

lightening _____

lightning _____

links _____

lynx _____

loch _____

lock _____

loot _____

lute _____

made _____

maid _____

magnate_____

magnet_____

maize_____

maze_____

mall_____

maul_____

manner_____

manor_____

marina_____

mariner_____

marshall_____

martial_____

mat_____

matte_____

me_____

mi_____

medal_____

meddle_____

meter _____

metre _____

mews _____

muse _____

might _____

mite _____

moose _____

mousse _____

moral _____

morale _____

muscle _____

mussel _____

naught _____

north _____

neice _____

Nice _____

panda _____

pander _____

pause _____

paws _____

peal _____

peel _____

pedal _____

peddle _____

penal _____

penile _____

plain _____

plane _____

pleas _____

please _____

pleural _____

plural _____

plum _____

plumb _____

pommel _____

pummel _____

precedent _____

president _____

premier _____

premiere _____

pries _____

prize _____

profit _____

prophet _____

quean _____

queen _____

rational _____

rationale _____

ray _____

re _____

read _____

red _____

read _____

reed _____

reek _____

wreak _____

rest _____

wrest _____

retch _____

wretch _____

rhyme _____

rime _____

road _____

rode _____

roc _____

rock _____

roes _____

rose _____

roomy _____

rheumy _____

root _____

route _____

rote _____

wrote _____

rye _____

wry _____

sail _____

sale _____

sane _____

seine _____

sax _____

saxe _____

scene _____

seen _____

scull _____

skull _____

sea _____

see _____

scene _____

seen _____

seam _____

seem _____

sewer _____

soar _____

shone _____

shun _____

sign _____

sine _____

sits _____

sitz _____

slate _____

sleight _____

slay _____

sleigh _____

slow _____

slough _____

snare _____

sneer _____

sodden _____

sudden _____

soot _____

suit _____

spacious _____

specious _____

spore _____

spoor _____

stake _____

steak _____

stalk _____

stork _____

stationary _____

stationery _____

storey _____

story _____

suite _____

sweet _____

27

taxes _____

taxis _____

teas _____

tease _____

theater _____

theatre _____

their _____

there _____

thigh _____

tie _____

thrash _____

trash _____

thread _____

tread _____

threw _____

through _____

throes _____

throws _____

throne _____

thrown _____

thyme _____

time _____

tide _____

tied _____

timber _____

timbre _____

time _____

thyme _____

tire _____

tyre _____

toad _____

towed _____

toes _____

tows _____

toot _____

tooth _____

tort _____

torte _____

tread _____

thread _____

trust _____

trussed _____

trustee _____

trusty _____

vice _____

vise _____

victuals _____

wittles _____

villain _____

villein _____

waist _____

waste _____

ware _____

wear _____

warrantee _____

warranty _____

wary _____

weary _____

wave _____

waive _____

weak _____

week _____

wean _____

ween _____

wind _____

wined _____

wood _____

would _____

wining _____

whining _____

wreath _____

wreathe _____

yoke _____

yolk _____

Add some more of your own.

Sometimes there are more than two words that have similar sounds. They come in triples, and quads and more as well.

Remember, there are many letters that have multiple sounds and many sounds that may be represented by different letters.

aerie _____

airy _____

eerie _____

air _____

ear _____

e'er _____

ere _____

heir _____

year _____

aye _____

eye _____

I _____

bare _____

bear _____

beer _____

bier _____

bight _____

bite _____

byte _____

boar _____

boer _____

boor _____

bore _____

borough _____

borrow _____

burrow _____

braise _____

brays _____

braze _____

but _____

butt _____

butte _____

buy _____

by _____

bye _____

cay_____

key_____

quay_____

cease_____

seas_____

sees_____

seize_____

cent_____

scent_____

sent_____

cite_____

sight_____

site_____

dais_____

days_____

daze_____

dare_____

dear_____

deer_____

decent _____

descent _____

dissent _____

do _____

doe _____

doh _____

dough _____

dew _____

do _____

due _____

earn _____

urn _____

yearn _____

fair _____

fare _____

fear _____

firs _____

furs _____

furze _____

flew _____

flu _____

flue _____

grays _____

graze _____

greys _____

grisly _____

gristly _____

grizzly _____

hair _____

hare _____

hear _____

here _____

hew _____

hugh _____

hue _____

hi _____

hie _____

high _____

knob _____

nob _____

nub _____

load _____

lode _____

lowed _____

lore _____

lower _____

lure _____

meat _____

meet _____

mete _____

more _____

moor _____

mower _____

nay _____

ne _____

nee _____

neigh _____

oar

o'er

ore

pair

pare

pear

peer

pier

palate

palette

pallet

peak

peek

pique

poor

pore

pour

praise

prays

preys

rain _____

reign _____

rein _____

raise _____

rays _____

raze _____

rapt _____

rapped _____

wrapped _____

rare _____

rear _____

rhea _____

rite _____

wright _____

write _____

road _____

rode _____

rowed _____

roes _____

rose _____

rows _____

rung _____

wrong _____

wrung _____

sew _____

so _____

soh _____

sow _____

share _____

shear _____

sheer _____

seoul _____

sole _____

soul _____

soar _____

sower _____

sewer _____

sou _____

sous _____

sue _____

stalk_____

stock _____

stork _____

stair _____

stare _____

steer _____

suede _____

swathe _____

swayed _____

tare _____

tear _____

tier _____

taught_____

taut _____

tort _____

torte _____

tea _____

tee _____

ti _____

team _____

teem _____

theme _____

titer _____

titre _____

tighter _____

toad _____

toed _____

towed _____

to _____

too _____

two _____

vane _____

vain _____

vein _____

wail _____

wale _____

weal _____

whale _____

ware _____

wear _____

where _____

way _____

weigh _____

whey _____

weather _____

wether _____

whether _____

wind _____

wined _____

whined _____

yore _____

your _____

you're _____

GRAMMAR PRIMER

Words are the building blocks of language and we are judged by the words we use. In the English language, there are many words that confuse us. There are words that have multiple meanings or usage: e.g. boxer: underwear; boxer: profession; boxer: dog. There are words that are spelt identically but have different sounds. These are **heteronyms**. e.g. rebel (verb): rebel (noun).There are words that sound identical but have different meanings, spelling, or origin. These are called **homonyms** e.g. lox; locks. Words of the same sound but different meanings are called **homophones** e.g. taxis, taxes.

There are **synonyms**, words similar in meaning, and **antonyms**, words denoting opposites. There are also **acronyms** and **eponyms** and **demonyms**. Language consists of words and symbols and the rules of language is called **grammar**. Every language has grammar. Without grammar, our communication would go awry.

There are many idioms in English; it has borrowed many words from many different sources, and it is continuously changing; thus, there are many pitfalls, where many words sound alike but are spelt differently, form plurals differently, form tenses differently, and one must use the skills of **listening** and **visualization** in order to communicate effectively. All this variety is due to **etymology**. In addition, there are many words that have very different meanings in different localities.

Many new words are formed by joining words, or by adding **affixes.** These affixes change concepts as they often have defined meanings. **Prefixes** are added at the beginning of words, while **suffixes** are added at the end of words and **medial affixes** are within words. A common suffix is 'er', which denotes a comparative, in adjectives, or a profession in nouns. The letter 'a' is also a common prefix. Note ad: adder; plumb: plumber; trophy: atrophy; toll: atoll.

Consonants are sometimes **doubled** when affixes are added.

There are twenty-six letters in the alphabet: a, e, i, o, and u are **vowels**. The remaining twenty-one are **consonants**. There are, however, over forty sounds in the language. In the word, *renege*, each 'e' has a different sound. Check the sound of '*ough*' in each of the following words*: bough, dough*, and *tough*, then the sounds of the letter 's' in *seas* and the sound of the letter 'o' in *one, bone, done,* and *gone*. However, occasionally, all five vowels may be silent, as well as some consonants, notably b, k and p.

Words may be classified as **parts of speech**. This is according to the role they play in sentences. Many words are used as more than one part of speech and have multiple meanings.

NOUN: the name of a person, place, thing or idea.

There are four kinds; abstract: an idea or quality, that one cannot touch. E.g. loyalty. Common and proper: e.g. a <u>dog</u> named <u>Rover</u>. Collective: a <u>school</u> of fish.

PRONOUN: used in place of a noun.

There are subject and object pronouns, personal and impersonal pronouns, interrogative pronouns, demonstrative pronouns and reflexive pronouns.

ADJECTIVE: describes a noun or pronoun. Used in comparisons: e.g. fast; faster; fastest.

VERB: says what a person or thing does; describes an action, (walk), event (rain), state (appear), or change (become).

ADVERB: modifies a verb, adjective or another adverb. They usually answer the question, to how, when, where, or why an action is done. The answers are sometimes adverbial phrases.

PREPOSITION; usually comes before a noun or pronoun, and shows the relationship between it and the rest of the sentence.

CONJUNCTION: used to connect words, phrases, clauses or sentences.

INTERJECTION: expresses a sudden feeling; an exclamation.

Nouns, verbs, adjectives and adverbs, sometimes change their form, primarily their endings, by the addition of suffixes, according to the role they play in a sentence. This is called **inflection**. E.g. honest: honesty; walk: walking. Nouns, verbs, and pronouns must **agree in number**. In English, only a few nouns and pronouns have gender. Many nouns in their plural form, end with this same letter.

In sentences, verbs and pronouns work together. They both **agree in number and person**. Some verbs need help so there are **auxiliary verbs**. Here is the present tense of two of them.

The verb 'to be'   The verb 'to have'

	Singular	Plural	Singular	Plural
1st Person	I am	We are	I have	We have
2nd Person	You are	You are	You have	You have
3rd Person	He, she, it, is	They are	He, she, it has	They have

The pronouns in the conjugations above are **Subject Pronouns**. They do the action. **Object pronouns** receive the action. Here are some object pronouns: me, us, you, him, her, it, and them. Subject and object pronouns usually refer to persons; so, they are, for the most part, **Personal Pronouns**. There are also **impersonal pronouns**, which are used in place of any nouns, except persons. There are also **Possessive pronouns**; mine, ours, yours, his, hers and theirs; and **reflexive pronouns**, used when the subject and object of the verb are the same person or thing, and they usually end with the suffix 'self'.

Verbs also have Voice; **active**, in which the subject does the action and **passive** in which the object receives the action. E.g. active voice: People judge us by the words we use. Passive voice: People are judged by the words they use. **Tense** indicates the time an action is done, or, whether or not it has been completed. The words "will" or "shall" usually indicates the future. The ending 'ing' usually denotes the action is ongoing. Many past tenses end with 'ed' and many past participles end with 'n'. But many English verbs are irregular. Here are some of them

Infinitive	Pres. Tense	Pres. Part	Past tense	Past Part
to be		being	was	been
to have	have	having	had	had
to cut	cut	cutting	cut	cut
to see	see	seeing	saw	seen
to fly	fly	flying	flew	flown
to get	get	getting	got	gotten
to go	go	going	went	gone
to sing	sing	singing	sang	sung
to come	come	coming	came	come
to do	do	doing	did	done
to speak	speak	speaking	spoke	spoken
to give	give	giving	gave	given
to sit	sit	sitting	sat	sat
to leave	leave	leaving	left	left
to take	take	taking	took	taken
to bring	bring	bringing	brought	brought
to buy	buy	buying	bought	bought

There are three main uses of the participles.

1. with the verbs 'to be' or 'to have' to form different tenses. She is leaving.
   He has left.

2. In the formation of verbal adjectives
   Broken promises: The spoken word:

3. In the formation of verbal nouns or gerunds
   The singing of the anthem: The cutting of the ribbon:

Here are some of the more common tenses.

The present (simple):	*She walks down the street*
The present continuous tense:	*She is walking down the street.*
The past (simple) tense:	*She walked down the street.*
The past continuous tense:	*She was walking down the street.*
The perfect tense:	*She has walked down the street.*
The future tense:	*She will walk down the street.*

PUNCTUATION

A **full stop** or **period** is used at the end of statements.

A **comma** is used to group words and phrases that belong together. It is also used to denote a slight pause, as with items in a series, and interjections.

A **colon** is used prior to a list of elements that rename or restate what has already been stated.

A **semicolon** is used to separate independent clauses or to divide a series of longer phrases.

An **apostrophe** is used to indicate ownership or possession, to form contractions, and to form the plural of a letter or number.

A **hyphen** separates the syllables of a single word, or joins multiple words.

Quotation marks are used around the exact words of a speaker; used with titles of songs, stories, chapter titles, short plays, episodes of television programs, magazine articles, and poems.

Question mark usually indicates a question, doubt, or uncertainty.

Exclamation mark used after a sudden feeling of emotion, or shouts.

Underlining is used with the titles of books, movies, newspapers, television programs, magazines and long plays.

MAXIMS

Explain the meanings of each if the statements listed below.

Be civil at all times, even if it hurts.

Always compete with, never against your opponent

Always do your best, at least one person will benefit

Always follow instructions in order to avoid anger or danger.

Always keep a list, a priority list.

Always respect your competitor or opponent.

Angry folk often hurt themselves, first.

Made in the USA
Charleston, SC
05 April 2013